# To Dream a Dream

## THE AMAZING LIFE OF

# Phillip Schofield

**BLAKE**

Published by Blake Paperbacks Ltd.
98-100 Great North Road, London N2 0NL, England

First published in Great Britain in 1992

ISBN 1-857820-06-1

Typeset by BMD Graphics, Hemel Hempstead

Printed by Grillford, Milton Keynes

Cover design by Graeme Andrew
Cover photograph and picture editing by David Hogan

1 3 5 7 9 10 8 6 4 2

For Marion and my parents – whose undiminished love and support has never ceased to amaze me!

# *Thanks*

My special thanks to John Blake for his unbeatable enthusiasm, Rosie Ries for her patience, Dave Hogan for his brilliant photographs, and Phillip Schofield for being such a fascinating subject.

Thanks also for supplying some great pictures to Alan Davidson, Alan Grisbrook, David Koppell, Syndication International and other kind friends.

# Foreword

I first met Phillip Schofield four years ago – and have since interviewed him probably more times than any other journalist.

Confident, amusing, thoughtful and intelligent, Phil has proved himself to be one of the most genuinely *nice* guys in showbusiness – though he won't thank me for saying that.

Typically, he wasn't keen on being the subject of a book – claiming with ludicrous modesty: "There's nothing about my life that would be of remote interest to anyone. I'm nobody special."

Millions of fans in Britain would disagree – and so do I.

Anyone who can present *two* hit TV shows, host his own Radio One programme, and star in a West End musical at the same time has to be special.

This is not a warts-and-all exposé of Phillip Schofield. There is, as his friends and family will tell you, nothing to expose.

It's simply the story of someone who dreamed of being a star – and achieved his dream.

And to use a cliché, it couldn't have happened to a nicer bloke.

# CHAPTER ONE

# The April Fool

Phillip Schofield's life didn't get off to a very impressive start. Oddly enough for a man who has made good timing and perfect delivery his byword, young Phillip got his birth hopelessly wrong.

Two hours wrong in fact. For, to his mother Pat's horror, he emerged at 2am on 1 April, 1962. Her first child was an April Fool. It may have been Mothers' Day, but Mrs Schofield was in no mood to celebrate. In fact Pat was so appalled that Phillip was an April Fool that she tried desperately to make the midwife change her son's date of birth for the records. But the midwife, who knew that this would be breaking the law, told the pleading mother that changing the date was out of the question.

Pat needn't have worried so much. Phillip grew to love the idea of being an annual fool and admits now that he would have been furious if his Mum had got her way.

He says: 'Mum tried desperately to have my date of birth altered to either 31 March or 2 April. She'd been keeping her fingers crossed for days that I wouldn't arrive on April Fool's Day but I was a difficult child even then and out I came!

'It should have been the greatest moment of Mum's life, having her first child, but all she could think about was me being an April Fool! She literally pleaded with the midwife to amend the records. She said only the two of them would know, and what would it matter. But the midwife wasn't having any of that. Mum was heartbroken.'

But Phil says being born on that day has been a barrel of laughs ever since. 'I would have been really cross if

Mum had changed my date of birth and I only found out about it later because it has been so much fun over the years. A lot of celebrities are April Fools, including the cricketer David Gower, Radio One DJ Annie Nightingale and Trevor from *Going Live*'s Trevor and Simon. The great advantage is that you never, ever get caught out by anybody else and you always have plenty of time to stitch up your friends.

'I did a beauty on my managers Russ Lindsay and Peter Powell once. I had just joined them and they were keen to get some business for me. Quite early on 1 April, I got a secretary friend of mine called Doreen to phone up their office pretending to be from the top advertising agency for Proctor and Gamble. She said she wanted to hire me for a new promotion called Phillip Schofield soap-on-a-rope.'

'Pete and Russ immediately saw a very large number of pound signs light up in their eyes, because TV adverts earn a lot of money. They were thinking, God we've only just taken Phil on and we've landed this already – it's incredible. They spent the rest of the day dreaming about how they were going to spend their cash!'

'That night I was hosting a party at my flat in Ealing. Halfway through the evening I stood up on a table and calmly announced that the Proctor and Gamble offer had in fact come from me.'

'Pete and Russ were devastated – inconsolable. As everyone else fell about laughing, they sat looking like guys who've just lost a million. It was hilarious.'

Phil admits he has, very occasionally, been April Fooled himself. He laughs: 'It takes a very clever person to get me because I have days to prepare for it, normally. But a couple of years ago I was getting ready to interview the environmentalist Jonathan Porritt for the Press Conference section on *Going Live*.'

Phillip, aged 6, on a Cornish beach.

A shining star in the making.

'At the very last minute they turned the cameras on to me and said I was going to be the subject. It was a total nightmare because I'd been given no time to prepare for it and all the kids asked me these incredibly awkward questions!'

Phillip's first eighteen months were spent in Oldham, then a very industrial town with thick, unhealthy air to match.

Pat Schofield knew it was not the place for her to bring up a baby son the day she looked outside her small family home to see the infant Phil playing in the garden covered in specks of black soot from the nearby factories. In her dreams she always visualised Phil on the idyllic beaches of Newquay, the beautiful Cornish seaside resort where she and her husband Brian had spent their honeymoon three years earlier. Seeing him covered in ugly black grime was the last straw, so within weeks the Schofields were making the 500-mile journey to set up home in Newquay.

They quickly found a small but well-appointed house close to the beach. And Brian, an experienced French polisher, found a job faster than he thought he would.

For the next few years Phil enjoyed the undivided and devoted attention of his Mum, who had, by now, got over her initial upset at his birthdate!

But lurking around the corner was a monster waiting to ruin Phil's blissful existence: school.

His first day at Trenance Infant School went well enough. He got up quickly, put on his new uniform and trotted off quite happily to join his first ever classmates. Six hours later, Pat found a smiling son waiting at the school gates to go home – full of stories about the fun he'd had. She was relieved and delighted. But the next morning a rather different Phillip was reluctant to get out of bed.

He recalls: 'When Mum tried to make me get up the

next day and put my uniform on again I looked at her in puzzlement and said: "I went yesterday, there's no reason to go again."

A shocked Pat had to drag Phil forcibly to class that day, and from then on Phil loathed school with a deep intensity.

He admits: 'It got so bad that Mum had to take me right into the building each morning and physically throw me through the classroom door. The teacher would then stand with her back to it so I couldn't run straight out again.'

'It was terrible and got worse and worse as the weeks went by. I thought school was the worst thing in the world and I behaved accordingly. They started sending me home at lunchtime because I was so disruptive to everyone else. They told Mum and Dad that they didn't want me during lunch because I made other children cry all the time!'

Phillip's anti-social antics soon made him a loner. He ended up spending most of his spare time sitting on his own in the playground, not talking to the other pupils.

He says: 'My Dad remembers walking past the school at lunchtime and seeing me underneath a tree all alone. I couldn't see the point of spending time talking with a whole load of strange children when my parents lived just up the road.'

'My early school experiences have had a long-term effect on me. It's only in recent years that I have felt comfortable in the company of people I don't know.'

Nor was he much better at home. When he was five he bit the tip off a pet rabbit's ear. It belonged to a friend who lived down the road and Phillip thought it was all very funny.

His mother didn't. Wincing at the memory, he admits: 'I still can't believe I did that. I was very small and when the rabbit nibbled me, I decided to nibble him back. 'But I overdid it and bit half his ear off. Mum was furious. She hit me all the way home – my feet didn't touch the ground, I was constantly in the air as she leathered me!'

He liked playing pranks on other kids too, particularly girls. One unsuspecting local female was chased down the street by a giggling Schofield, being repeatedly clubbed with a fiendish home-made weapon: a bamboo stick with a piece of dog mess thoughtfully attached to the tip.

Fortunately diversion was on its way. When he was seven years old, Phil got a baby brother called Tim.

Phil has vivid memories of Tim's arrival. 'My father was down at the hospital and my aunt was looking after me at home. I really hadn't got a clue what was going on, other than that it was all rather odd and exciting.'

'It was a dark night in March and all of a sudden we heard a knock at the lounge window, and I looked up to see my Dad's face peering through the darkness and shouting: "it's a boy!"'

'Then he jumped into his car again and vanished.'

To accommodate their expanding family, Brian and Pat moved to a bigger house in Newquay and set themselves up in business running a guesthouse.

The Schofields were a happy family unit. Phil recalls special occasions like Christmas and birthdays fondly.

He says: 'One year Mum and Dad gave me a train set they had spent weeks and weeks making for me. It had houses and stations made from kits and trees – and level crossings that Dad built and painted.'

'It was a huge thing, the size of a big coffee table. And I had two steam trains called Polly and Nelly, who kept me occupied for hours. The next year they gave me a zoo, and by the time I was ten I had almost a whole city.'

# CHAPTER TWO

# The Candy Floss Man

Brother Tim proved to be the perfect distraction for Phil, who was already harbouring dreams of being a radio star.

At the age of ten he started writing letters to the BBC, asking all sorts of things about broadcasting. Shrewd for someone so young, he typed his letters so they wouldn't reveal his age – and he got detailed replies from DJs, producers and other senior BBC employees.

One of the kindest replies came from the then queen of radio, Annie Nightingale, He says: 'A lot of the top DJs didn't bother replying at all, and most of those who did sent a standard printed letter. But Annie sent me a hand-written note offering genuinely helpful advice and encouragement. I have never forgotten that and I make sure when people write to me now that I don't fob them off with a duff reply.'

'I remember how important these things are when you are young.'

Tim, meanwhile, was the ideal interview subject – even at the tender age of three.

Phil laughs: 'I had made my mind up that I wanted to be a top DJ who would spend all his time interviewing big stars.'

'I used to race around interviewing Tim about everything I could think of. I'm pretty sure his first words were "No comment", because he learnt very quickly that if he said that I would stop hassling him!'

Phil's enthusiasm for his new career dream knew no bounds. He devoted hours to building model radio and television studios out of cardboard boxes and performing mock

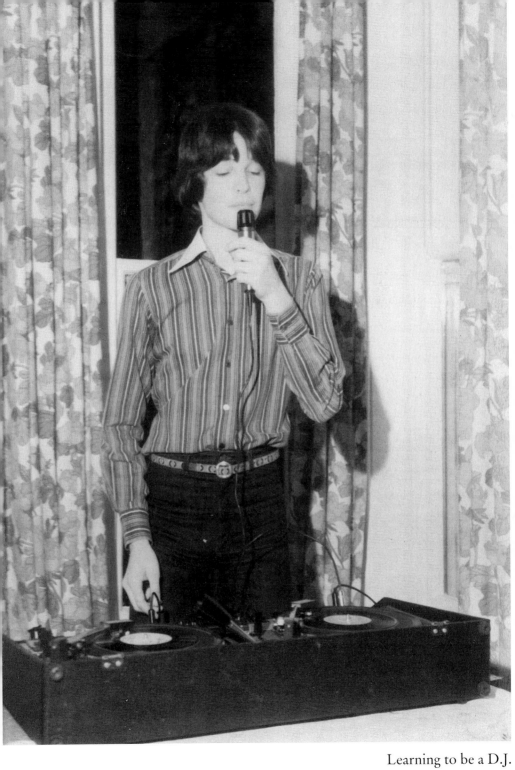

Learning to be a D.J.

Happy family - mum, dad and brother Tim.

road shows and gigs in his bedroom.

He says: 'My family must have all thought I'd gone mad, but they never showed it. They were incredibly tolerant.'

'I was determined from an early age that I was going to be a broadcaster. I can remember sitting on one glorious sunny afternoon with the seagulls whizzing overhead listening to the radio. It was such a wonderful feeling.

'Apart from a very brief period at infants' school when I wanted to be a grave digger, I never thought about doing anything else.'

Phil was also showing a keen interest in drama – an interest that was to pay off handsomely some twenty years later. He landed the coveted part of Prince Charming in Crantock Junior School's annual pantomime at the Cosy Nook Theatre. His excellent performance not only won him the envy of his classmates, it also enabled him to kiss the most sought after girl in school, Louise Tucker, at least once a night!

He recalls: 'She was the only reason I wanted to be the prince – all the boys in school fancied her and they were furious that I got to kiss her every night.'

Mum Pat watched every show proudly from the wings. She says: 'His teacher felt Phillip was too good for the part. They expected kids of his age to make a few mistakes but Phillip didn't make any.'

'He *was* Prince Charming. The very minute he walked on stage everyone treated him like a prince. And he genuinely expected everyone to bow to him!'

'I thought then that if he ever had the opportunity to go on stage again he'd do it without any problem at all. He was a natural.'

School, however, was still rearing its ugly head.

Phil moved from Crantock Junior School to Tretherran

Senior School – where his general behaviour didn't improve.

He admits: 'I was not so much a bad pupil as mischievous. I did a lot of naughty things which I never got caught doing – thereby avoiding the cane.'

'One of my favourite little tricks was a home-made device made of fuse wire, magnesium tape, tinfoil and wax. When placed in the right way and in conjunction with an overhead projector the effect was magnificent: A brilliant white light and a very, very big bang.'

His attitude towards other children was still grossly anti-social.

He recalls: 'I used to get into quite a few fights. I took on the school bully one day, with the whole school turning out to see us scrapping away in the playground. After a lot of frantic thrashing we ended up honours even. Because there was no out and out winner we came out of it with a sort of mutual respect.

'I remember him well because he had this huge family, all of whom used to bully people. I won't say his name because I know for a fact that he still has a huge family...'

Phillip's early hero was Noel Edmonds. He says: 'Noel was brilliant and I dreamed that one day I would do a show like his.'

As he got older, Phil developed the charm and personality that has made him so popular now. With his new-found charisma came friends. But one thing continued to bother him, almost to the point of being an obsession: his size.

Phil was very slim, and not very tall. And he developed what he describes now as a "silly complex" about it.

He says: 'It used to get me down a lot and I went around wanting to be bigger than I was all the time.

'I started eating more and more to try and put on weight but nothing happened. To this day, it doesn't matter

Shazam was a huge break.

Dynamic D.J. at work.

what I eat; I never put on weight. I wish I could market my diet secret, but I've no idea why I'm so lucky.'

Nor was Phil happy with his looks generally. He admits: 'I was very disappointed with the way I looked. I hated my face, although I didn't have spots or anything. I just got it into my head that I was an ugly teenager and that was enough to make my life miserable a lot of the time.'

'Looking back, I think the main problem was that I was quite desperately untrendy!'

Strangely, he has not kept contact with any of his childhood pals.

He says: 'I had two really good mates and we used to go everywhere together. But an odd number is always a mistake. There was always one of us who was left out.'

'If I could change anything in my life it would be that threesome, because it wrecked my upbringing. You always tried to make sure that when you were in you would help the guy who was out. But the truth is that you made bloody sure the odd one out felt as damned awful as he could possibly feel.'

'People always say keep your schoolfriends and they will be the best friends that you ever have. But I was always left out during the summer holidays and as a result I haven't kept in touch with any of them.'

With plenty of time to himself, Phil concentrated on fulfilling his dream of being a DJ.

The Radio One Roadshow would always come to Newquay, where stars like Alan 'Fluff' Freeman, Ed Stewart, Noel Edmonds and Paul Burnett would host the live shows.

Standing at the front looking on eagerly was Phillip Schofield – destined one day to host his own Roadshow in Newquay.

He says: 'I saw each and every one of the Roadshows. I would go down first thing in the morning to watch them prepare the shows and I'd stay on at the end to see them pull it all down.'

'I made sure I was in the front row, though unlike all those around me the very last thing I wanted was to get up on stage and make a complete plonker of myself.'

'Instead, I waited and carried on writing furiously to the DJs, the producers and anyone else who might listen to my pleas for a job.'

Phil's first real attempt to get into deejaying was going to cost money, so he got himself a load of holiday jobs to save some cash.

He says: 'Because Newquay was a seaside resort, all the jobs were connected to tourism.'

'My first job was making candy floss on the seafront. It went very well for two weeks, then the weather turned a bit and it became wet and windy. This caused all sorts of problems with the floss-making machine which I was operating.'

'To my horror it started gushing out floss all over the place. I ran out into the street with floss covering me from head to toe, it was up my nose, between my toes, in my hair – everywhere.'

'And more worryingly it was also over all the customers who had the misfortune to be in the shop at the time.'

'The boss of the shop went mad – calling me all the names under the sun and saying I was the most useless candy floss maker he had encountered in his entire life. He sacked me on the spot, which was a shame because I had to walk a mile home with floss all over me – and sticking fast!'

'I was only earning about 50p an hour then, which hardly seems worth it, does it?'

Phil soon progressed to a more lucrative and less hazardous job: running an ice cream kiosk.

16

He says: 'It was a brilliant place to get revenge on all those rude tourists who assume everyone else has to be nice to them just because they are on holiday. You can't believe how unbelievably rude some people were. In seaside resorts some holidaymakers treat local people like slaves and expect them to wait on them hand and foot.'

'But I was ready for them. If a thug came up to the kiosk and demanded a can of Coke in a surly voice I would reach into my cupboard and produce one I'd tampered with earlier. It would have been shaken, beaten, kicked around and generally turned into a fizzy bomb.'

'The yob would disappear round the corner, then I'd hear this explosion and see a large geyser of brown liquid shooting twenty feet into the air. Usually, less then ten seconds later, the man would be back demanding another can. It was always a pleasure giving these morons a free one after that.'

Phil's most entertaining job was working on a remote-controlled tank park. He spent the winter making the eighteen-inch tanks and the summer supervising the parks.

He says: 'They were quite powerful things, but sometimes the battery tape would erode and the batteries would touch the tanks' aluminium bases. At that point the tanks would usually catch fire and all hell would break loose as I desperately tried to put it out.'

'The funny thing was that the public would look at this blazing tank just a few yards away and say: "Crikey, that's realistic!"'

Phil's radio ambitions soon got him a job as a DJ in a local disco and he ended up working three hotels in Newquay throughout a summer. Meanwhile he continued to bombard the BBC with application forms and eventually he turned up trumps.

After passing six O-levels and a 'terrible CSE' in maths,

he was considering doing A-levels when the Beeb wrote offering him a job. Phil had no hesitation – he was on his way.

# CHAPTER THREE

# The Worst of Times

Phillip Schofield's career began somewhat inauspiciously as a bookings clerk in the BBC's Outside Broadcasting Department.

He had just passed his seventeenth birthday and made the move to London with a mixture of trepidation and excitement.

Phil's salary was just £3500 a year, but he didn't mind. The truth is that he would have *paid* to do the job, just to get the chance to learn his trade.

He admits: 'It was the greatest job in the world as far as I was concerned. My whole ambition was to be a DJ and this was the first rung.'

'It was the BBC, and that meant dozens of famous people were wandering around all the time. Because I had an official pass, I was able to walk around just about wherever I liked and not be stopped. I used to take full advantage of this and walk up to the DJs to ask them all the burning questions I had always wanted to ask.'

'It was a fabulous launching pad – and I didn't waste the chance.'

Phil got on well with his workmates – who quickly introduced their youthful new boy from Cornwall to the pleasures of real ale.

Phil admits: 'I spent much of the two years consuming vast quantities of beer, which was great fun.'

But just as Phil started casting his eyes towards a more prominent job at the Beeb, he was sent reeling by a bombshell from his family.

His parents phoned him one morning at the small one-bedroom flat he was renting in West London to tell him they were emigrating to New Zealand – and that he was coming too.

Phil was devastated. He had spent seven years trying to get a job at the BBC, now he'd got one and he was about to give it up. For weeks he was inconsolable.

He admits now: 'I couldn't believe it. My first reaction was that my parents wanted to go on holiday there and I was pleased at the idea. I knew Dad had always wanted to go to New Zealand. But when they said it was a permanent move I was stunned.'

'I had a good job, and some great mates. Why the hell would I want to move 12,000 miles to New Zealand? I was nineteen and it was the ultimate nightmare. But what it boiled down to was a simple choice between throwing away everything I had worked so hard for, or being thousands of miles away from parents.'

'I decided that I couldn't do without them.'

On the day of the departure, Phil was so angry he couldn't speak to anyone. He recalls: 'I was a pig, I wouldn't talk, I wouldn't eat, I wouldn't do anything.'

'It was undoubtedly the worst day of my life.'

His malaise continued for weeks after the Schofields arrived in New Zealand, but he soon found a job on a local radio station, made some new friends and started to enjoy himself.

Amazingly, their next-door neighbours shared the same surname, and the two girls were exactly the same age as Phil and Tim. For a year, they hung out together – though the friendship never crossed over into romance.

Then tragedy struck. The older sister, who had become Phil's best friend in New Zealand, found a lump in her leg one morning and three weeks later she was dead. Phil says it was one of the saddest episodes in his life.

Phillip's wonderful family have always backed him.

The rising, young heart-throb.

'She was a lovely girl. She wasn't my girlfriend but we were virtually inseparable. We lived next door to each other and shared the same name.'

'For months we had great fun together. She never drank, never smoked and was incredibly athletic. But one day she found this lump in her leg and that was it.'

'It was so terribly sudden, and so awful. I remember hearing that she had died and thinking, "My God, she's only nineteen."'

The devastating blow hit Phil badly, but he threw himself into his work to try and get over the loss of his friend.

His winning combination of boyish charm and highly competent technique made him an instant hit with New Zealanders, and he was soon offered his first TV job: presenting a pop show called *Shazam*. Ironically, it was his namesake neighbours who persuaded him to go for the job.

He says: 'Telly was a complete accident for me. I had been quite happy doing radio work, and on the odd occasion when I had considered TV, I was told my English accent wouldn't be suitable.'

'Then the next-door Scholfields pointed out an advert in the paper for an audition for this new pop show *Shazam*. My parents were very supportive and said I should give it a go, but I said I wanted to be on radio not the TV and was utterly convinced I would be useless on the box. Eventually they persuaded me and I got the job!'

'To this day I will maintain that it was a pure fluke.'

Phil soon became a star – by interviewing rock legends like Elton John.

He says: 'I did a one-hour special with Elton, which was amazing. He was going through his ultra-flamboyant stage and the stuff he was telling me about the money he spends was incredible.'

'It remains one of my career highlights, but I have to

say that the best subject I have ever inteviewed wasn't Elton, but Donny Osmond. He really got into the spirit of things and was a lot of fun.'

'Midge Ure too was great, such a smashing bloke to meet.'

But just when it seemed that his life couldn't be any better, another tragedy struck: his father Brian, who had developed a boundless appetite for huge local steaks, had a heart attack.

Phil will never forget the dreadful moment when he saw his Dad collapse on the living-room floor of their three-bedroom family home in Christchurch. Nor will Brian ever forget Phil's involvement – because he saved his life.

Phil says: 'Whatever happens to me in the future, nothing will compare to the sheer terror I felt then. We were all sitting around watching TV and chatting when Dad started complaining of chest pains. A few seconds later he dropped like a stone on to the carpet.'

'We all panicked, Mum was distraught and screaming for help. Tim was too shocked to move, and I flipped completely. To see the very fabric of your family disintegrating in front of your eyes like that was ghastly.'

'We are such a close family and nothing like this had ever happened to us.'

As Brian lay unconscious, Phil knew he had to do something to bring him back to life. His mind raced through various possiblities – including baring the lamp wire and electrocuting himself.

Thankfully, he quickly realised how dangerous that would be. Phil has never been particularly religious, but he believes God helped him at that precise moment.

'I am sure there was some divine intervention, because suddenly the basic rudiments of first aid came back to me. I put him into the correct position and started whacking

*Above*: Phillip's first car, a Sunbeam Rapier.
*Below*: Clowning about in the kitchen.

Phillip gets canned.

him on the chest. I hit him so hard that I burst several blood vessels in my arms.

'Dad was black and blue by the time they got him to hospital from where my blows had landed. I'd given myself three minutes to bring him round and nothing happened for two minutes. I thought that I'd blown it, but then he made a noise and I knew he was coming round. It felt like a miracle – I couldn't begin to describe the emotions which went through my mind that second.'

The ambulance screeched to a halt outside two minutes later and the ambulancemen rushed in to find Brian in a semi-conscious state. They took one look at Phil and told him: 'Carry on thumping him, son, until we get our paddles and zapper out.'

Phil says: 'I wasn't doing it exactly right but it was good enough as far as they were concerned.'

Five minutes later they had revived Brian enough to get him into an ambulance. They told Phil as they left: 'Congratulations, you have saved your father's life.' They were to later give him a certificate confirming it, but Phil dismisses the praise.

He says: 'All I cared about was Dad. I chased the ambulance so fast to the hospital in my car that I actually beat them there.'

'Dad came round properly a few hours later, but couldn't remember a thing. He wasn't in any pain from his heart. But he was in agony from where I had been belting him!'

Brian, who had been very fit up until that day, lost his sense of smell and taste for a year afterwards – a small price to pay as far as he was concerned. But the incident had a permanent effect on Phil. He admits he still can't watch a heart-attack scene on TV or at the cinema without turning away.

He says: 'I am reminded of Dad immediately and that is just too emotional for me. But the ironic thing is that I believe everybody *should* watch those sort of scenes on telly because there is no doubt in my mind that they helped me save my Dad's life.'

'I had never had any formal first aid training – the little I did know I picked up from watching the box. And it came back to me.'

Amazingly, Brian turned on the radio by his bedside when he came round, only to hear an interview with a man who claimed it was totally unnecessary to have a heart attack in this day and age!

Phil says: 'We had to laugh; there are seven radio stations in Auckland and he had to tune into that one at that particular time. But in fact Dad listened to the whole show and he was fascinated.

'The man was called Ross Horn and he had written a book called *The New Health Revolution* which has become Dad's bible now. 'It was all about diet: what you should and shouldn't eat.'

'At the time Dad loved tucking into huge New Zealand steaks and other meats. He was not stressed and he was constantly active. But it taught him how important diet is and Dad is now a vegan and fitter than me.'

'He is fifty-six now and you would never believe that he ever had a heart attack.'

Phil knows that neither he nor any of the family will ever erase that awful memory from their minds.

He says: 'Dad and I know what happened but it's not something we like to dwell on. I think we are both just very grateful for the fact that he survived it.'

'It was the worst experience of my life and I will never forget it as long as I live.'

# CHAPTER FOUR

# On the Way Up

Phil's career started taking off around this time. He got his own radio show, became a celebrity hosting *Shazam* and then got handed his ultimate accolade: hosting the New Zealand music awards in 1984.

He still rates this as one of the highlights of his career.

'They wanted me to present an award at first and I said I was a bit too busy. Then a few hours later they came back and asked if I would present the whole hour-and-a-half long show.'

'I was thrilled because it was such a long, live show and my first really big break. I planned it meticulously and wrote my own script. It went really well and I was very relieved.'

Phil was enjoying himself away from work, too. He had built up a good circle of friends and taken up hobbies like powerboat racing and mini car racing.

The latter almost ended his career, and life.

He recalls: 'I was really into racing the minis and got to a pretty good standard. But one afternoon I had a crash and got trapped inside the car. My safety harness was jammed and the mini suddenly caught fire.'

'It was a very frightening moment, seeing those flames leaping up all over the place and not being able to get out. It felt like an age before the fire boys raced over and put it out. Though in reality it was probably only a few seconds.'

Phil spent a total of four years in New Zealand – and fell in love wth his adopted country. When the time came to come back to Britain, he did so with a heavy heart.

He still holds a dual passport and admits: 'A part of me will always be there. It is such a friendly, open place – where the people are so kind and helpful. And they take a great pride in me, which is such a nice thing.'

To Phil's undisguised fury, he did an interview for a national newspaper back in the UK which misquoted him as saying he would be bored out of his brains if he ever went back to New Zealand.

He says bitterly: 'It was *The Times Educational Supplement* of all papers, and they wanted to do a nice, happy, travel article with me.

'They asked me where I was going for my summer holiday and I said I knew I would be bored, so I would be going back to New Zealand.'

'When the piece appeared, it made out that I was not looking forward to going back because it would be so boring – the complete opposite of what I had said. My quotes appeared in all the New Zealand papers and I got into serious trouble with some of my friends, who were understandably very concerned about what they read I had been saying.'

'All they have ever expected from me over there is the same loyalty they have shown me and I am well aware what a great contribution that country has made to my career. People rang me from all over the world complaining about the story.'

'I had to apologise all the time. Eventually I got so angry that I phoned the news editor of the *New Zealand Herald* and asked him if he would put a piece in stating how I really felt. He promised he would but of course that wasn't such big news and it never appeared.'

Phil reckons he would still get heckled over that article if he went back now, two years later. He says: 'They have

Launching Going Live with Sarah Greene.

With Jason Donovan.

long memories over there and I wouldn't blame them for being offended. Nothing fires up that very proud nation more than people knocking them – especially the English.'

Within four months of arriving back in Britain, Phil had landed a prime job back with the BBC – they were impressed by the tapes he showed them of his work in New Zealand. He was given a unique job which was specially created for him: linkman on children's TV. He took up the challenge with relish, if some nervousness.

But Phillip's first afternoon in the linkman job nearly didn't happen at all.

With less than five minutes to go before he was due to make his first link, Phil was standing on a fire escape outside the BBC building. He was smoking furiously, and very, very scared.

He remembers: 'I stood there shaking like a leaf because I knew that this was the moment I had been waiting for all my life. This was the day that would decide whether I could hack it in the big time.'

'I was thinking to myself, "If I blow this, I'm finished, it's all over." I was sweating and fretting, it was awful.'

At that moment, his producer, Ian Stubbs, appeared, looking equally agitated, on the fire escape.

'I think he thought I was going to jump,' says Phil. 'But when he realised I was just nervous, he started cracking jokes to try and calm me down a bit. I can't remember what they were but they must have worked because I did feel better by the end of them!'

Phil was due on at the end of *Blue Peter* – one of the least reliable shows for ending on time in BBC history. Typically, they ended a few minutes early, so Phil was ordered on to cover the two-minute gap as best he could.

He says: 'Biddy Baxter was the *Blue Peter* presenter at the time and she was as near to God as you could get.

Eye eye...what's going on here then?

'Allo, 'allo, welcome to zee Europeans.

She didn't care if the show over-ran or under-ran – what she said went.

'I couldn't believe my bad luck when they under-ran. It meant I had to ad lib from the start.

'I remember seeing the *Blue Peter* presenters all gathering, which is always a sign that they are about to finish. And my producer Ian rushed in saying, "Sorry mate – you're on."

'I thought, "Christ, what the hell am I going to do?"

'In the end I filled most of the time with a picture of Simon Groom and a giant sea slug, while I rambled on about nothing. I started off quite calm and ended up a wreck, but I got through it and that was a great relief.'

'I definitely earned my colours that day – they felt that if I could cope with that on my first day then I could cope with just about everything.'

Phil soon got into his new job – which he adored.

'I was the first linkman at that time and so there was a real pioneer spirit. That led to some great TV – and some almighty cock-ups. I literally had the power at my fingertips to do anything I liked, which was a constant worry, as you can imagine.'

'One afternoon, they changed the output on my camera and I couldn't get myself back on screen. In my efforts to retrieve my face I managed to get all sorts of strange things, including a spooling tape, a picture of the globe and a large clock, on screen – everything, in fact, except me.

'Eventually I did get my face back – and we promptly lost the sound! It was a total fiasco, which lasted for a good minute. It was a Friday, so I had the whole weekend looming in front of me and the last ten seconds were complete silence.'

'As my nightmare finished the lady talking in my ear came on and said: "Sorry Phil darling, there is nothing I can do to help you..."

'As the credits rolled, all I could hear was this thundering noise, which was my editor charging down the corridor towards me. He grabbed me in a terrible rage and took me straight into a side video room where he made me sit through the whole thing again.'

'He asked me, "Do you realise that was one of the worst things ever perpetrated on the BBC?"'

'Everyone was so stony-faced and shocked that I was sure I was about to be sacked. But at that moment, the then head of BBC presentation, a brilliant Scottish guy called Malcolm Walker, burst into the room and said, "That was the most wonderful piece of television I have ever seen. It was very funny and quite disastrous."'

'Because he was the boss everyone started laughing with him and within seconds the whole room was heaving with laughter.'

'I had escaped. But I still had to apologise to all the viewers on the following Monday morning. I came clean and said it had all been a nightmare. I owe Malcolm Walker a lot.'

# CHAPTER FIVE

# The Agony Uncle

Phil was soon earning a decent pay packet, and bought himself a smart one-bedroom bachelor pad in Ealing, West London.

But he still pined for New Zealand and needed a re-minder of those days to keep him happy. It came in the form of crickets.

A good friend of Phil's in New Zealand kept tarantula spiders and crickets as a hobby. As soon as he heard the familiar sound of crickets together, Phil recalled the tropical nights in New Zealand again and he promptly went out and bought a huge load of crickets and put them in his bedroom.

He took great care of them and treated them like any other pet. They lulled him to sleep most nights – and he only got rid of them when he started getting up so early that they were keeping him awake!

He says: 'In New Zealand you could open the window and hear the crickets singing. It was very soothing. I started off with about a hundred but I didn't realise they were cannibals and they all started eating each other.'

As Phil's popularity grew, it soon became obvious that he was destined for greater things on the telly. Producers recognised his amazing rapport with children – and the fact that adults liked him too. Parents saw him as a perfect role model for their kids.

After finishing his link one afternoon, he was sum-moned to see the top brass of the BBC's children's TV department and offered the job of hosting a new Saturday morning show called *Going Live*. It would follow in the tradition of Noel Edmonds's *Swap Shop* – and be a totally live programme.

It was what Phillip had spent many a night dreaming about. He accepted immediately.

*Going Live* quickly became the most popular youth show on the box, drawing millions of children every Saturday. It made Phillip Schofield a household name in the process.

He says: 'There is nothing else on British TV anything like *Going Live*. It is so varied, so long and so live that literally anything can happen and usually does.'

'The attitude that Sarah Greene and I have always taken is that we will try anything and if it works it works – if it doesn't, it doesn't. It rarely gets out of control, because Sarah and I both know how far to go. But that's not to say things don't go wrong, because they do, all the time.'

Phil admits he watched a video of his first ever *Going Live* recently and almost collapsed.

He laughs: 'It was so bad, embarrassingly awful to watch again. God knows why they let me do another one after that but they did and things did get better!'

Phil has become a hero figure for millions of children in Britain – and thousands of them write to him every week for advice, turning him into an agony uncle.

He knows how important this responsibility is, and doesn't take it lightly.

'I find it incredibly flattering that these kids trust me enough to want my advice on things.'

'Most of them want tips on boyfriends or girlfriends, what they can do about their spots, being overweight, things like that. But I get about five or six letters a month which deal with far more serious issues and it is those that I devote a lot of time to.

'I have had children telling me they are suffering horrific abuse, or saying that they have an incurable disease.

When I read letters like that, I get a lump in my throat and I feel desperately inadequate. I wouldn't ever reply to them offering advice. Instead, I refer the letters to specialists and write back to the children, telling them what I have done. I keep an eye out for what happens to them after that, too, because it's all to easy to forget about them.'

'I couldn't bear the thought that children might suffer from my giving them duff advice. Spots and girlfriends I can advise on without worrying too much, because I've been through all that. And I will give advice on things like contraception which is not obviously life-threatening. But the serious cases need far more sensitive handling.'

Phil will never forget one little girl whose parents wrote to him saying she had died from cancer and that the very last words she ever said were his name, Phillip Schofield.

'I couldn't believe what I was reading. I thought, "My God Phil – how could you possibly hold such an important place in someone's life?" It was the highest compliment I will ever be paid – a fantastic honour which I, sadly, will never get a chance to thank her for.'

'I wrote to her parents and sent flowers to the funeral but I felt so helpless, really. There was nothing I could say or do to make them feel better. They were so desperately upset.'

Another heart-breaking letter came from a young girl's parents who said that she was a great fan of Phil's and would love to meet him – though she was dying from leukaemia in hospital.

He recalls: 'The parents knew she was dying but she didn't. I went down to the hospital where she was, one afternoon, and spent a few hours with her. We chatted away about all sorts of things and she was such a lovely little girl. She was just the prettiest little thing you have ever seen.'

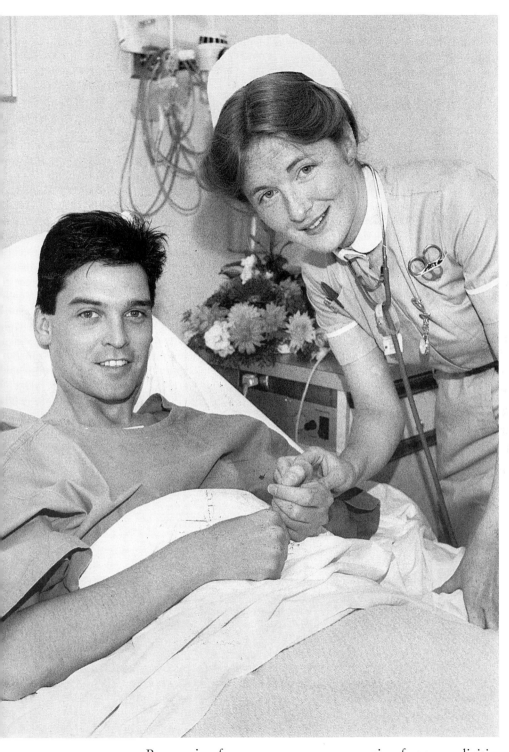

Recovering from an emergency operation for appendicitis.

With Caron Keating

'All the time I was talking to her, I couldn't believe that she was dying. She didn't look very ill, although she was at the time. We watched a few videos and then she wanted *Neighbours* on, so we watched that together. Then her friend came round as well and we had a great laugh.'

'When the time came to leave I told her to come and see me at *Going Live* when she was better. But I knew that she was never going to get better, that there was no hope for her at all – and so did her parents.

'It was so incredibly sad, especially as on the outside she looked so well.'

Phil said goodbye to the girl and her parents and walked to his car in the hospital car park. As he sat inside, he burst into tears.

He recalls; 'It was just too much for me. I am not a doctor and I am not able to cope with that sort of thing emotionally.

'I sat there and wept buckets. I was so upset, and so angry that this should happen to a girl like this. What had she ever done to deserve what had happened to her?'

'I kept in touch with her parents and she got better, then worse, and then they wrote to me two weeks after we met to say that she had died. I wept buckets after that. I was very, very emotional and I still get choked whenever I think about her.'

'I phoned her parents to tell them how sorry I was and they were so grateful for what I had done. So grateful for what, though? Who wouldn't have done what I did under those circumstances?'

Phil makes a handful of visits to seriously ill children each year. He always goes in secret – and refuses to allow photographers anywhere near him.

He says: 'I will sit with a sick child for as long as it takes. But I don't want to read about hero Phil in the papers. There is nothing heroic about it. A lot of stars do it and they never get any credit for it.

'Why should you? It's such a small thing to do, and yet it means so much to the person concerned.'

There have also been some happy stories involving sick children.

Phil says: 'We have had some lovely endings to what could have been tragedies. I remember one girl who had been run over and was in a coma. Her parents asked me to record a tape so they could play it to her. I made this tape and promised her that if she came round again she could come and see me at *Going Live.*'

'When they played it she came round. It was fantastic. She got better and better and eventually got out of hospital. When I heard this we got her straight round to the show and she had a great time.'

'It was a real joy.'

Phil admits he would love to be a Dad himself.

He says: 'I think I would be a very good father. I genuinely like kids and seem to get on with them very well.

'I know quite a few people in my business who spend so much time working that they never have time for anything else and that is sad.'

# CHAPTER SIX

# *All You Need is Love*

One of the most laughable accusations in showbusiness is that Phillip Schofield might be gay.

The rumours, which tend to haunt any unmarried TV personality who prefers not to show off his girlfriends in public, have dogged Phil on and off for years. But anyone who knows the handsome presenter treats them with the ridicule they deserve.

For the truth is that Phil has hardly ever been *without* a girlfriend, making him one of the most eligible bachelors in Britain.

Since he sneaked his first kiss at the age of five from a young lady called Susan, whom he chased into a giant Wendy House, Phil has pursued women with enthusiasm.

His first real love was Jackie, a girl he met at Crantock Junior School when he was fourteen – and whom he dated for more than a year.

For a good-looking young man, Newquay was a veritable paradise – with hundreds of girls flocking to the seaside resort for holidays. Phil, like most of his mates, took full advantage. He recalls the moment he lost his virginity well: 'I was fifteen; no one forgets, do they?'

'It happened in the sand dunes of Newquay beach. I remember the girl very well; her name began with L – but that's all I'm saying. I still see her occasionally and don't want to embarrass her.'

'She knows that she was my first!'

Phil's lovelife blossomed when he moved with his family to New Zealand. The combination of his English accent and that cheeky grin lured many a girl into agreeing to a date.

An early Antipodean girlfriend was, ironically, a half-Russian called Marika. She was a television floor manager working on the set of *Shazam* and Phil admits he only asked her out because all the other men in the building fancied her and he wanted to be the first to take her on a date.

Unfortunately Marika's Russian upbringing quickly became a major problem to their relationship. The chief drawback was her father's habit of toasting every word anyone spoke with the traditional slugs of vodka.

Phil recalls: 'Marika was my first serious relationship.'

'I asked her out because I wanted to put all the other guys' noses out of joint. But evenings at her house proved to be rather too challenging for me. Marika's father would insist on toasting everything from the cook to the youth of the world, even our socks sometimes – always in neat vodka. By the end of the evening the guy would be paralytic and we'd be out of our brains too.'

'Dinner used to be equally hazardous. Exploding tomatoes, bloated to the point of bursting in salt water, and raw fish used to be regulars on the menu. It turned into a bit of a nightmare.'

The romance ended in a series of rows. Phil says: 'Marika was a real cow to me in the end.'

'But although I was upset I didn't let it get to me or affect my work at all. Nothing, no traumas, no nightmares, nothing ever interferes with work as far as I am concerned. I pride myself on being able to keep my private and professional life totally separate.'

But Phil admits that as their relationship lapsed into bitterness, he did play one naughty trick on Marika.

He says: 'I'm not very proud of it now but at the time I was very pleased with myself. I was hosting a radio show

Going...going...gone! Who said Going Live was kids' stuff?

in New Zealand at the time and dedicated John Waite's song *Ain't Missing You at All* to her.

'It was a really cheap jibe but that was how I felt at the time.'

Phil was choked about the bust-up but he didn't have a long wait before he found someone new to catch his eye. It happened at the party after the aforementioned music awards show. Phil was sipping a glass of champagne and holding a plate of food when he spotted one of the show's backing dancers a few feet away. He was knocked out by the leggy beauty and could hardly take his eyes off her. Her name was Fenella Bathfield.

Phil says: 'I was still getting over Marika and I was in no mood to start another relationship so soon afterwards. I was on cloud nine because the show had gone really well and I had come off stage on a real high. I was wandering around with this plate full of food, which I didn't want to eat because my stomach was churning so much.

'Then I saw Fenella and my mouth dropped so far I thought I was going to swallow her. She was absolutely the most perfect woman I had ever seen, and for the first time in my life I fell hopelessly in love at first sight. I was head over heels about her from that moment – it was an amazing feeling.'

Phil went over and introduced himself to the stunning brunette who had captured his heart.

She was not overly impressed. He laughs: 'Unfortunately Fenella thought I was a bit of a berk because I was on TV.'

'But I was quite pleased about that, because I knew then that she would like me for who I am, not what I did – assuming I could persuade her.'

Fenella had gone to the party with her boyfriend Steve – but he left early when he saw how well she and Phil were getting on.

He says: 'He seemed a rather boring guy and we hit it off straight away without thinking about Steve. Eventually he got the message and went home early. Fenella and I went back to the hotel I was staying in for a coffee and talked for what seemed like hours. But it was all above board and she went home eventually, with me managing to get her phone number out of her.'

The next day an eager Phil was on the phone first thing, pleading with Fenella to have dinner with him.

She readily agreed – but there was one rather large problem: he lived in Auckland and she lived 100 miles away in Wellington.

For the next few months Phil spent every penny he had on flying to and from Wellington.

He says: 'Nobody drives in New Zealand and trains are museum pieces. The only way we were going to be able to sustain our relationship was for me to keep catching the plane!'

For two years they dated. They grew so close that Phil admits he came close to proposing marriage. Then came a bombshell that would almost certainly put an immediate end to their romance. Phil decided his future lay in Britain.

He knew that Fenella wouldn't give up her job as a dancer, and that if he went he would go alone. But he also knew that he had to make the break if he was ever going to fulfil his burning ambition to be a major personality.

He will never forget the day he had to tell Fenella he was leaving.

He says: 'She just burst into tears – and so did I.'

'But while I never asked her to pack in her dancing and come with me, she never begged me to stay either. It was a terrible wrench at the time – Fenella was the only

Ballet dancer Fenella Bathfield lets it all hang out!

woman I had ever felt so strongly about and we were very happy together.

'I believe there have to be fireworks from the start in a relationship for it to work and we had plenty of those. There has to be mutual trust and the sure knowledge that you can cope with anything together.'

'It hurt me a lot that the one time it really looked like working out it didn't.'

Phil was sad as he made the 12,000-mile trip back to London. He knew he was leaving behind possibly the greatest love of his life – and having to cope with his new life on his own was not a very heartening prospect. He bought the small one-bedroom flat in Ealing – but admits he was 'as lonely as hell' for the first few months.

He found himself missing Fenella and they wrote to each other constantly, even exchanging the odd expensive telephone call. But both of them started seeing other people and slowly they tried to forget each other.

Phil went out for months with Gloria Hunniford's gorgeous daughter Caron Keating – who went on to present *Blue Peter*. They were very happy together, but Phil knew in his heart that Fenella was the girl for him.

After two years, Phil went back to New Zealand for a holiday and their romance sparked back into life almost immediately. For the next four years, Phil and Fenella continued a bizarre 12,000-mile love affair that amazed their friends.

Each year, either Phil would fly to New Zealand or Fenella would come to see him in Britain. When they got together, it was pure unadulterated passion from start to finish.

Phil admits: 'The problem was that we both wanted the relationship to continue, but neither of us was prepared to make the ultimate sacrifce and move to the other's country.

'I think if we had done, the magic may have quickly disappeared and we would have realised the awful truth about each other. But because we only saw each other for a few weeks a year it was an incredibly exciting, and hugely enjoyable experience.'

They both carried on seeing other people in between visits, but in the build-up to the big reunion, their hearts would start to beat and Phil confesses: 'I could hardly wait for Fenella to walk down the aeroplane steps. The feeling of anticipation would start three days before she arrived and by the time we clapped eyes on each other again it was quite something.'

Their relationship was incredibly passionate, but incredibly fragile at the same time. Phil says now that they both knew it would either end in marriage or they would have to split up. In the end, it was the latter.

On her last visit in 1990, Fenella and Phil had an even better time than usual. They spent most of their days holding romantic picnics in fields. Their sexual attraction for each other was as strong as ever. But both of them knew deep down that this was going to be their swansong.

Phil says: 'We loved each other very much. But it got to the stage where we realised we couldn't go on the way we were. We were in danger of ending up like the couple in *When Harry Met Sally* and doing this when we were seventy.'

'Our last four weeks together were wonderful, but when the time came to say goodbye we looked at each other and knew instinctively that it was over. We knew we had been as lucky as we could be without ruining our very special friendship.'

Their last night together was especially memorable. Phil took Fenella to a celebrity party in London and photographers besieged them all night. Unfortunately, Fenella's

Time to face the music...with Stephanie Lowe

With mum.

low-cut black dress slipped a little too low as the wine flowed and gave one snapper rather too much to photograph. Horrified, Phil saw the situation and tried desperately to cover Fenella up before the flash went off. He failed – and millions of newspaper readers were treated the next morning to a picture of Phillip Schofield's girlfriend showing off her right breast!

He recalls: 'She didn't think anyone had got the picture, but I saw the look on one of their faces and I knew he had. He was grinning from ear to ear!'

'Fenella flew back the next morning and only knew about the picture when I told her on the phone a few days later. She was appalled!'

They said goodbye with a few tears and a few loving hugs. A couple of months later Fenella phoned Phil at 6.30 am to tell him she was engaged to a New Zealand lawyer. He was not surprised, but admits to a little heart sickness at the news.

He says: 'I knew she had been seeing this guy for some time and that she was very happy with him. We had not planned another meeting and both realised that there was no chance of the romance between us being rekindled.'

'I was thrilled to bits when she told me she was getting married. I even spoke to the guy and congratulated him, wishing him all the best. He was very good, considering what he knew about me and Fenella, and said he'd love to invite me round for dinner with them the next time I was in New Zealand.'

'I can't see him asking me to stay the night somehow . . .'

Phil says he feels no bitterness about Fenella's decision to wed someone else.

'I don't feel any anger, sadness or bitterness. We are still great friends and I am genuinely happy for her. I don't dwell on what might have happened if we had stayed together. Perhaps we would have married – who knows?

'We never had enough time together to get bored, so we never really discovered the things that might have irritated us about each other. I think I would be a very difficult person to live with. I can be bad-tempered and I have a short fuse sometimes. I like my own way and I'm always asking others: "Why?"

'The great thing about us was that we never argued once. We had a very passionate relationship but never rowed about anything. We had some crazy times and she will always be very special to me.'

'We both agreed to see other people when we were apart, so it was inevitable that one day one of us would meet someone a bit special.'

'My lasting memory will be how the passion would smoulder away then we'd pour a can of petrol over it and go mad for four weeks. It was all very naughty – and very nice. We had a ball.'

As Phil's popularity grew, so did his appeal to women. They would bombard him with saucy letters at *Going Live* and Radio One. Most were from young schoolgirls who'd developed a harmless crush on the handsome star. But some were from randy housewives and mothers who had taken a fancy to his boyish charm.

He laughs: 'I get a very big mailbag most weeks and a lot of the letters are from females pledging their undying love for me. I take them with a pinch of salt because the letters would soon dry up if I disappeared off the telly.'

'It's the clean cut TV image they are attracted to, not the real me.'

'Some mums write to me with some very explicit suggestions about what they would like to do with me. Their imaginations are extremely creative!'

But he's never been tempted to take up any of the offers. Phil admits there is no bigger turn-off than a woman throwing herself at him.

He says: 'I've been out with a lot of women. But I am fairly guarded.'

'I've had a few nightmare dates where everything had been going really well until the girl said something like, "Well, I never thought I'd be sitting here having dinner with . . ."

'When I hear those words I ask for the bill immediately and get away as soon as I can. You've never seen anyone move so fast.'

'But I can usually tell if a girl's motives are suspect. I have a very close circle of friends and they can all spot the groupies a mile off.'

'Every time I come out of Television Centre there are a few girls who have waited hours just to see me. Sometimes it will have been really cold and they are half frozen. But much as I would like to offer them a lift to the tube station in my car I know that I can't take that risk.'

'Sadly I have to be very guarded about what I do in those situations. I remember one pretty girl who asked me if she could have her picture taken with me. She put her arm round me and I gave her a peck on the cheek. As she and her friend walked off down the road, I heard her say: "That will look great in one of these Sunday papers." '

At the moment women needn't bother trying to lure Phil. For the last eight months he has been blissfully in love with a blonde TV presenter called Stephanie Lowe.

They knew each other for years before going out together – and now she shares Phil's luxury West London home. Friends say it is only a matter of time before they wed.

Phil says: 'I am considering marriage, obviously. I am thirty years old, financially secure – and I'd love to have children.'

About ninety per cent of my friends are either married or getting married and I have no desire to be left on the shelf. I've got a big house with plenty of room for a wife and a wee Schofield.'

Before meeting Stephanie he admitted: 'It will take a very determined woman to break down my shields. I've been dumped a few times because the girl said she never saw me and when she did I was never very emotional. That's true – I do work seven days a week.'

'But I am quite looking forward to the day when I can walk into my management office and tell them to tear up my diary because I'm getting married.'

Now that looks increasingly likely.

Phil's dream girl would be someone like Demi Moore.

He says: 'I have fancied Demi for a long time. I was one of the originals. Me and my mate Paul fell in love with her after watching *Blame It on Rio*. When *Ghost* came out last year and everyone started drooling over her we were thinking, "For God's sake – she's been around for years".'

'I love Meg Ryan and Julia Roberts too. But that's all lust fantasy really, I couldn't imagine having an intellectual relationship with them – or wanting one for that matter. If it was brains I was after I would go for someone like Whoopi Goldberg, who has always made me laugh.'

'But I'm very fickle – I fall in love with women I see in magazines. I've always been the sort of man who believes he is just about to meet the great love of his life.'

Friends reckon Phil may have met that woman in Stephanie. One thing is for sure – he definitely *isn't* gay!!

He laughs: 'Because I have always guarded my private life very closely, these sort of rumours are bound to fly around. But I've got one thing to say to anyone who says things like that – bollocks!'

n the town with Stephanie Lowe

*Above*: Two technicolor dream-boats
*Right*: Champion of the world

*eft:* Phillip with Fenella Bathfield
*bove:* Spot the dummy

*Left*: A man of many parts
*Above*: Phillip gets sex machined

With little Bernice Foster and Mrs Thatcher

# CHAPTER SEVEN

# Those Crazy, Crazy Nights

If there is one thing that is likely to ruffle even Phillip Schofield's ultra-thick skin, it's the sneering accusation that he is too squeaky clean to be true.

He admits: 'It really gets to me sometimes that because I am not seen to behave badly in public there must be something wrong with me.'

'It's just very boring – the truth is that when I am not in the public eye I behave exactly like any other thirty-year-old bachelor. It's just that I am very careful not to do anything that might cause a parent to think I am unsuitable to be a role model for their child.'

Friends of Phil's confirm that he likes to get rip-roaringly drunk, has an eye for the ladies, and enjoys a good prank.

He laughs: 'If people knew the real me they would probably be horrified. I have had some extremely dodgy nights. I've been so drunk that I've ended up sleeping on tube trains, crashing out in offices, on floors, in fact anywhere I fall over. I have got home sometimes and the next morning had absolutely no recollection of where I'd been or what I'd done or indeed how I got back. It's quite worrying really, isn't it!'

'But the funny thing is that no matter how drunk I've been, I always seem to take my contact lenses out before I go to bed. That never ceases to amaze me.'

One of Phil's most memorable nights on the booze came when his mate Peter Powell got married to Anthea Turner and had a stag night the week before for his close mates.

Stars, including Phil, Gary Davies and Andy Crane all joined in the marathon knees-up, which ended with Peter being chained, wearing just his underpants, to Chelsea Bridge.

Phil was one of the chief perpetrators. He says: 'It was a fantastic night. Totally wild and crazy.'

'Most of us who went have to be pretty careful about getting too drunk because of our jobs and the fact that there might be a photographer lurking somewhere. But this night we just went for it and got completely smashed.'

'It started in a Fulham pub, where we sank a ridiculous amount of alcohol. The record plugger Ollie Smallwood and I organised it and it could not have gone better.'

'We all piled into a fifty-two seater coach we had hired for the night and drove to Chelsea Bridge, where we de-bagged Pete and handcuffed him to the bridge. A few of us made sure he was well and truly done by pouring what was left of the champagne all over him. It was a freezing cold January evening and he was soaking – but I think the drink made him immune to what was happening. We all jumped back in the coach and as a final gesture dropped our trousers and mooned at him. There were photographers there who I am pretty sure caught that moment, but the pictures never appeared for some reason.

'Pete eventually had to be cut free by firemen, and the police were not too amused to start with. They took him half naked down to the station but let him go after he promised to pay £300 to charity!'

Phil admits to a penchant for wine and whisky.

He says: 'My favourite drink is definitely Jack Daniels and orange juice. And I love New Zealand wines – especially one called Cloudy Bay. But I steer clear of red wine, it leaves you with such a thick head the next day.'

Phil avoids nightclubs – for the simple reason that he

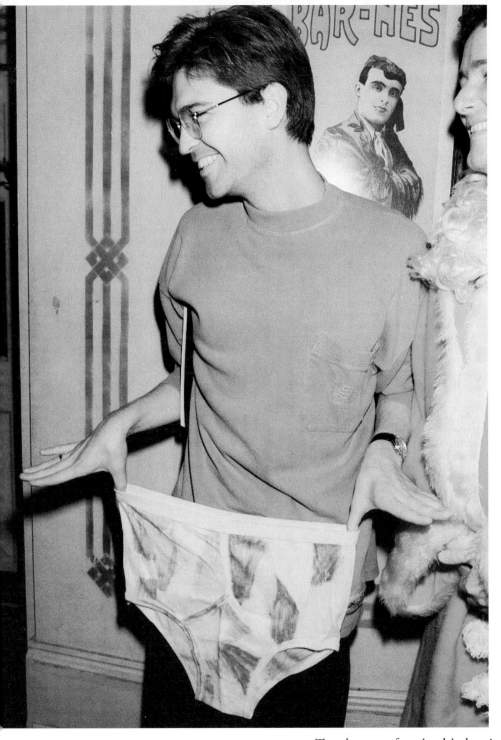

Try these on for size big boy!

Stitching up Peter Powell

doesn't like them much. He would much rather spend an evening in a nice restaurant with friends.

He says; 'I like food, and there is nothing better than a good meal with good wine and good friends. My favourite restaurant is the new Langham Hilton, opposite the Radio One offices in Regent Street. It is like going back in time there.'

'There is also a great little place near my home where they serve American soft-shelled crabs. I go there just to eat that meal and they have it ready for me as soon as I walk though the door. If it's not on the menu I just don't eat anything, it's as simple as that. It's such a wonderful dish – you eat everything including the shell and the claws. It's served with lashings of garlic. The first time I ate it it almost blew my mind – it was like a strange, culinary sexual experience.'

Despite his growing success and fortune, Phil shuns the usual trappings of stardom.

He explains: 'I may earn a lot of money, but I never lose sight of the fact that I am just an entertainer, nothing more serious than that.'

'Most people do far more important things than me. I don't save lives, I don't guide 'planes into airports, I don't fix burst water pipes or put out fires. I am a TV entertainer. But for some reason people expect you to behave like you are Liz Taylor or something.'

'I remember one day when I was booked to open a shopping centre. The organisers sent me the biggest white Rolls Royce you have ever seen to pick me up. I took one look at this disgusting thing and refused to step into it.'

'My manager Russ Lindsay was with me and he said I had to use it; I couldn't send it back. So I slunk into the back seat and tried to hide. Then we stopped at these traffic lights in Ealing and a few people spotted me. To my utter horror the Rolls then stalled at the lights. The driver tried to restart it and then lost his temper completely. He was screaming abuse at the car and stamping his feet like a deranged madman He was calling it a bastard, son of a bitch, everything – all at the top of his voice.'

'More and more people were gathering round to see this débâcle, and can you believe that in the end I had to get out of the Rolls and help this bloke *push* it round the corner. People were looking at me in total amazement. I was so humiliated that when we had stopped pushing, I told Russ to take me straight back to the house and we went in his Sierra in the end. I just could not come to terms with the Rolls at all.'

'I was forced to drive in one to another do once and I hated it so much that I ended up driving back in the PR girl's battered old Orion.'

# CHAPTER EIGHT

# My Pot of Gold

Phil never forgets what it was like to have no money – and admits: 'I don't think there is a person in Britain who is not feeling the pinch. I have a mortgage. I didn't buy my house outright as people might like to think. I bought at the top end of the market three years ago and it probably isn't worth anything like what I paid for it then.'

'Thankfully I am able to afford the repayments reasonably comfortably and I love the house so much that I don't want to sell it anyway. But I am never blasé about my earnings. I have seen too many people in this business get their fingers burned because they didn't look after their finances properly. You have to be in the business a very long time before you have made enough money to stop worrying about it.'

'The one thing a lot of personalities forget about is that dreaded three letter word *tax*. I am lucky enough to have a great accountant and a great lawyer. All I have to worry about is the work.'

'Money is nice, obviously – it makes life a lot easier. Having said that, I can remember having absolutely no money at all and pressing my nose up against restaurant windows, wondering how on earth people could afford such prices. But I was having just as much fun then as I do now with a bigger wage and a bigger house.'

'I would be a liar if I said money didn't help. I have used my pot a few times; it's there for emergencies and I like the fact that I am able to do little things for my brother and my family that they couldn't afford to do otherwise.'

Phil admits that sometimes his money has caused problems for him.

He says: 'Me and my brother Tim get on brilliantly. He runs a record shop in Newquay and does very well. I remember one Mothers' Day when I got carried away and bought Mum a huge bouquet of flowers. Tim sent her flowers as well, but as many as he could afford, which obviously wasn't as much.'

'I felt awful about that and spoke to him the next day to apologise. It was a very stupid thing to do. But he does get a few benefits from being my brother – like free records, T-shirts and concert tickets!'

With his hectic schedule, Phil doesn't get a lot of time for holidays. But when he does, he has a great time.

'I like going somewhere exotic – my best holidays were in Thailand and the Seychelles.'

At his three-bedroom home in West London he amuses himself by listening to music, reading and playing his Nintendo Gameboy.

He says: 'My musical tastes are pretty varied. I like REM, Deacon Blue, Hue and Cry – and I was very upset when Then Jericho split up because I really liked them.'

'My all time favourite album would have to be *Love Over Gold* by Dire Straits. It brings back memories of an absolutely wonderful evening which I will not talk about!'

Phil's only real self-indulgence is clothes. He admits he takes a great pride in his appearance – and he's canny when it comes to buying them too.'

He says; 'I have a couple of friendly companies who help me out. I go round to their factories and they give me clothes for nothing.'

'Everyone who appears on TV has a friendly company. I doubt anyone could afford to keep a presentable image on telly without having a large amount of free clothes.'

A special cuddle for singing coach, Kate Young.

Looking dangerous.

Phil's by-word is routine. He wakes every morning to the sound of *four* alarm clocks – to ensure he doesn't oversleep. He then has a fixed morning order – he shaves, cleans his teeth, showers, does his hair, gets dressed, picks up his car keys and leaves.

Phil admits that his enthusiasm to get to work is triggered by a simple fact – he is always worried that someone might come along and nick his job.

He smiles: 'My father worked hard all his life as a French polisher for not much money and so I feel very lucky. But then I think how hard I've worked for the last sixteen years and I reckon I deserve some success. I still work six or seven days a week and I never get bored.'

'I have never felt overworked – I could do more if I really pushed myself. I am very organised because you have to be in this business.'

'If you are stressed because of some domestic problem it will affect your work. And that is the kiss of death in showbusiness.'

He has always had a weekly cleaning lady in to wash and iron his clothes and clear his pad up. But he insists that there is always a fairly "lived in" look.

It all sounds very boring, doesn't it? But that's the way Phil wants people to think he lives his life, very organised with nothing left to chance.

But don't ever take his incredibly clean lifestyle too literally.

He says: 'Until recently I smoked twenty cigarettes a day. I gave them up to do *Joseph* and it wasn't easy.'

'And I like to get drunk occasionally and have a good time. If you are invited to my annual fireworks party you are guaranteed to have fun. It makes me a little annoyed when I hear people describe me as squeaky clean because I'm really not.

'After Peter Powell's stag night I got a few letters saying how absolutely disgusting my behaviour had been, and how ashamed I should be feeling. And you know what I think of them? They can all naff off.'

Perhaps the biggest test of Phil's legendary calm on live TV came during the 1991 Smash Hits pop awards. A band called Carter The Unstoppable Sex Machine decided that getting the chance to perform their single *After The Watershed* in front of fifteen million viewers was too good an opportunity to waste. As they were faded out twenty seconds early, guitarist Leslie Carter charged across the stage and threw himself at Schofield, who was preparing to announce the next act. Uproar followed as security men leaped on stage to pull the crazed pop rebel off a stunned Phil – while the TV cameras panned to the other side of the stage.

Amazingly, Phil reacted to this ugly stunt as if nothing had happened. He stood up, dusted himself down – flashed his biggest smile and just carried on with the show.

But afterwards he confessed: 'It was the most incredible thing that has ever happened to me on stage. This band were annoyed that they were being cut short, but that is very common on live shows where things over-run constantly. One of them threw his microphone into the orchestra pit, narrowly avoiding the musicians. It was a very stupid thing to do and I made a crack like "Oh, that was original." Suddenly, out of the corner of my eye, I noticed this guy charging towards me at high speed.'

'He walloped me with an excellent flying rugby tackle and sent me crashing to the ground. I knew the cameras were rolling, and that millions of people were watching this bizarre scene, so I was determined not to give this guy the attention he obviously wanted.'

'He was throwing his hands around all over the place,

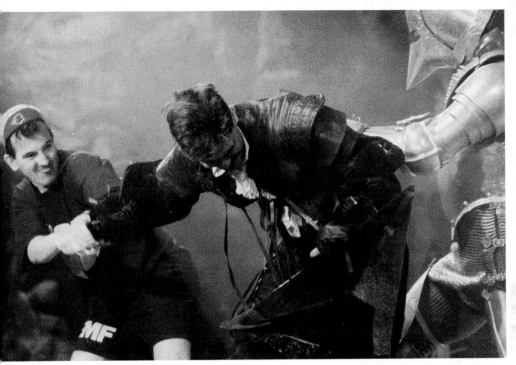

Getting to grips with Carter The Unstoppable Sex Machine.

though I am still not sure whether he actually hit me or not. I was pretty dazed, but I got up and finished the show as he was dragged away.'

'The next day, Carter got the headlines they wanted, but probably signed their death warrant as far as appearing on live television is concerned. Attacking a presenter on stage is bad enough, but attacking Phillip Schofield was an almost treasonable offence. One paper summed it up by saying; "It was a bit like belting the Queen Mother – you just don't do that sort of thing."

What it proved though was one conclusive thing – Phil is a supreme professional.

Only once has that professionalism slipped and a bit of the real Phillip Schofield emerged.

He was doing a Radio One Roadshow in Weston-super-Mare, in Avon and Bros stars Matt and Luke Goss were his guests. A huge crowd of about 40,000 youngsters had turned up, and some of them reacted to Matt by jeering and booing. The twenty-three-year-old singer had recently hit the headlines because of money troubles – and some of the comments being shouted were very unpleasant.

Phil appealed with the crowd to give Matt a warm reception – but to no avail. As he spoke, an egg flew towards the stage and landed on a young handicapped girl sitting at the front. Phil saw this and exploded with fury. Ignoring the fact that he was on live radio, he grabbed the microphone, turned to the audience and shouted at the top of his voice: 'I would like to tell the person who threw that egg that you are just a w*****.'

The effect was stunning. Forty-thousand people watched the supposedly squeaky clean star in blank amazement.

Phil didn't apologise – although a Radio One spokesman said they were sorry if anyone was offended by the swear word, which was not in the end broadcast thanks to a very quick-witted technician.

Phil said later: 'I saw this egg cash down on this poor little girl and I felt total fury at the person who had done it. No-one further back than the first few rows would have seen where the egg landed, so they must have thought I'd finally flipped. But I defy anyone to see something like that happen and not to react like I did. It was probably the only time I have lost my rag like that when parents and children are in the crowd, but I suspect I would do the same tomorrow.'

# The Amazing Technicolour Dream

By October 1991, Phillip Schofield's career was at an all-time high.

He presented a prime time Radio One show, hosted the ever popular *Going Live*, and his more adult orientated travel show *Schofield's Europe* had proved he could appeal to an audience of any age.

But one afternoon he took a phone call that was to make even those achievements pale into insignificance.

Phil had just got home from doing *Going Live* and was putting his feet up for an hour when his manager Russ Lindsay rang to tell him some astounding news: Andrew Lloyd-Webber was looking for a new heart-throb to replace Jason Donovan in his hit musical *Joseph and the Amazing Technicolour Dreamcoat*. He wanted Phil to go for an audition.

There was just one question Russ needed to ask rather urgently: "Can you sing?"

Phil recalls: 'Russ said he had something to tell me that was going to take some believing. When he told me what it was I nearly fell off the sofa. It was the hottest musical in the West End and I had never sung a note in public.'

'The idea of me taking over from Jason was ridiculous – wasn't it? Russ laughed down the phone and asked me if I could sing. I said I'd performed some excellent solos in the bath but that was about it.

'I was convinced the whole thing was a wind-up – Russ getting revenge for all the April Fool pranks I've pulled on him. But two days later I was on stage at the London Palladium, shaking like a leaf, and doing a preliminary audition for the show's musical director Michael Dixon.'

Three days later, Phil was invited back for a final test in front of Lloyd-Webber himself.

He won't forget that in a hurry: 'For those three days I was in a total panic. I became a nervous wreck, which was totally alien to my normal outlook on professional matters.'

'I'm the calmest man in the world but here I was losing my filofax, driving out of multi-storey car parks with my briefcase on the roof and generally being a bungling fool.'

Phil admits he was so scared on the way to the Lyric Theatre in Hammersmith for his final audition that he couldn't speak.

He said: 'The last time I had sung was in a pantomime at junior school.'

'When I arrived Andrew said, "Hello – bit of a surprise, isn't it!"

'I was ushered up on stage and given a song book. The pianist asked me what I'd like top do as a warm-up and I said I had no idea because I had never warmed up before. So Andrew just told me to sing the first few bars of "Any Dream Will Do" to check the piano. Once I started, I just carried on to the end, cocking up at least one of the verses.

'Andew looked up and said, '"So you can hear the piano then..."

'There was what I can only describe as a very polite ripple of applause, but by the time I'd finished the second song, "Close Every Door", I felt a lot better – I thought I'd done reasonably well.'

'But nobody gave any indication how *he* thought. Andrew just shook my hand and said he would be in touch with his answer the next day.'

That day was a Saturday and Phillip crowded into his manager Peter Powell's West London house with a few

The Amazing Technicolor Dream Coat.

Portrait of two Josephs.

mates to wait for the call.

It never came.

He admits: 'I thought I had blown it. We were watching the rugby world cup final on TV and every time the phone rang everyone leaped up into the air and screamed. It was a nightmare. I tried to be nonchalant about it, but inside I was in a turmoil.'

'Eventually it was clear Andrew was not going to ring so I went home to another sleepless night, thinking I hadn't got the part after all.'

For a man used to constant success, the thought of failure was almost too painful to bear. It was an agonising night.

But the next morning, a car drew up at Phil's elegant home. It was Peter Powell's and it was 9.30 am.

Phil knew instinctively that he was the bearer of good news.

He said: 'I knew as soon as I saw Pete's car that I had got the part. There was no way Pete would have come over at that hour to tell me bad news.'

'He just stood at my front door and said: "Do you really want to do this?"

'I said, "yes". Then he asked me again and I said, "yes" again.'

'"Well in that case," he said, "you've got the job".'

The two great mates hugged each other in the cold October air. They knew they were about to embark on the most exciting time of their careers.

First, Phil had to break the news to his friends and family – few of whom had been aware of his recent auditions.

He said: 'I hardly told anyone in case I was useless and didn't get past the first audition. A few people like my parents and Sarah Greene knew – and they were absolutely thrilled when I told them I was going to be taking over from Jason.'

'Sarah had told me before I went for the audition that I had always planned every aspect of my life meticulously. Nothing was left to chance – it was all carefully detailed. Now was the time for me to take a risk – she told me to go for it.'

'As for my other friends – they reacted in one of three ways. They couldn't speak, they stuttered and sat down or they simply burst out laughing. I think everyone thought Andrew had finally flipped.'

One of the most incredulous people was Jason Donovan – who had known Phil since he first starred in *Neighbours*.

He was astonished.

Phil said: 'I rang Jason and he told me he had been asked to guess who had landed the part of his stand-in. He was told it was someone he knew, but that didn't help.

'Jason said he rattled off every name he could think of but they were all wrong. Eventually the awful truth dawned on him and he said, "Oh my God – not Schofield!"'

But when he had time for the news to sink in, Jason was thrilled.

He said: 'Phil's a good friend of mine and I couldn't think of a better guy to take over from me. He may not be a singer but I knew he would put everything he had into making the role work. Phil is a very professional guy.'

Andrew Lloyd-Webber, who has made some of the world's greatest musical stars, knew he too was taking a gamble. But that was something he was not only used to – but good at. He recalled that his own fourteen-year-old daughter, Imogen, helped him make the choice.

'Imogen is a great fan of Phillip and thinks he is wonderful. There were quite a few people in the frame for the part, including Jason's former *Neighbours* colleague, Craig McLachlan and American actor, Johnny Depp.'

How fickle is fate. The changing fortunes of Joseph

'But Phillip just seemed to me to be the most obvious person to have a stab. People said I was taking a massive gamble – one of the biggest of my career. But I took a big gamble with Jason and he worked superbly. He turned *Joseph* into one of my most successful shows.'

'I had been interviewed by Phil on *Going Live* a few times and he always impressed me with the calm way he handled live TV. I knew he was looking to branch out into other areas of the business and when I invited him to audition he was surprisingly good.'

'I told him to have a few singing lessons and come back a week later and he did even better. I didn't want a Jason clone. I wanted a new Joseph and Phil proved to me at the audition that he could sing.'

'He had everything to lose and he was not daft enough to risk everything if he didn't think he could do it. And neither, for that matter, was I.'

News of Phil's appointment got to the papers within minutes of Powell and Lindsay signing the £10,000 a week deal for Phil.

The news certainly caused a storm. And most people were saying the same thing: "Has Lloyd-Webber gone stark raving bonkers?"

Phil was determined to make the doubters eat their words.

Within days he had torn up his diary, cancelled everything he'd booked for the next three months, and thrown himself into a gruelling fitness and voice-training routine.

Jason proved to be invaluable. He recommended Phil to his own singing teacher, Mary Hammond. She quickly had him singing from the stomach, not the throat. And gradually his voice got stronger and stronger. His physique was the next problem. To be brutally frank, Phil was a bit of a wimp and in less than eight weeks he was facing the less than wonderful prospect of unveiling his puny body to the world in just a loin cloth.

Again on Jason's advice, he headed for the gym and got his own personal regime organised. He was soon lifting weights, doing tough aerobics, skipping and running.

And his body, though not exactly turning into Rambo, was getting muscular enough for Phil to stop worrying about his appearance.

He cut out drinking altogether, sticking to Perrier and fresh fruit juice. And he tried to be in bed early most nights to save energy and help build up stamina for the gruelling task ahead.

He said: 'Jason admitted he was knackered by doing eight shows a week – and he was very fit! When I told him I intended to carry on doing my radio and TV shows he looked at me and shook his head, telling me I was mad. But I was determined to make it work.'

# Superstar

Two months later, Phil had reached dress rehearsal stage and knew that the most important moment of his life was just twenty-four hours away.

As he sang his heart out for the umpteenth time to an empty Palladium, just one thing kept going through his mind: 'What happens if I go to sing and nothing comes out?'

The rehearsal went well. The superbly talented *Joseph* cast, including former *Brookside* star David Easter and the wonderful narrator Linzi Hartley, were so good he had to be only OK to get through. In fact he was excellent.

Andrew Lloyd-Webber left the theatre that night a happy man. He was confident his gamble was about to pay off handsomely.

The following night, the Palladium had reached first-night fever. Excited schoolgirls fought with Mums and older students to get through the mass of people gathering in the foyer. Dozens of celebrities turned out to support Phil, including *Bread*'s Jonathan Morris, Sarah Greene, Gloria Hunniford and Simon Mayo.

There wasn't a ticket to be had – and touts were having a field day, getting up to £100 for top tickets.

The press were there in force, too – everyone from the tabloids to America's ABC Radio. Most importantly, as far as the debutant was concerned, the Schofield family had made the trip, too – Mum Pat, Dad Brian and brother Tim. As ever, they were there to support their boy, the boy they were so desperately proud of.

With minutes to go, Phil was sitting in his dressing

room, surrounded by good-luck messages from stars and friends. Everyone from Frank Sinatra to Liz Taylor had sat in that same room.

It was funny, thought Phil, he bet they were just as nervous as he was...

As he contemplated, a messenger knocked on the door: 'Five minutes, Mr Schofield.'

As he was gently lowered fifteen feet on to the stage, the 2,000-strong audience erupted into spontaneous wild applause. It was the sort of ovation an Olympic athlete would expect after smashing a world record.

Phil recalled: 'I couldn't believe the reaction. I was so nervous my tongue dried up and I was convinced nothing was going to come out. It felt like I was either getting married or going to the doctor. But the cheering gave me such a lift that when I began to sing it all just flooded out'

For Lloyd-Webber, sitting with new wife Madeleine Gurdon and movie mogul Robert Stigwood, it was a triumphant moment. As the cheering got bigger, so did the millionaire producer's grin. He knew instantly that his gamble had worked. He also knew that in Phillip Schofield he had found another major stage star.

To journalists who had gleefully flocked to witness golden boy Phillip's inevitable demise, first impressions were pure shock. The voice and the acting, were sensational. And it was not just the fans who thought this.

After an understandably nervous first half, Phillip was catching his breath backstage during the interval when Andrew Lloyd-Webber suddenly appeared. What he had to say stunned Schofield into silence: 'You were marvellous Phillip, just wonderful. How would you like to take the job over full-time when Jason leaves in May?'

Phillip turned to his managers Russ and Peter – both grinning from ear to ear. They knew that this was a licence

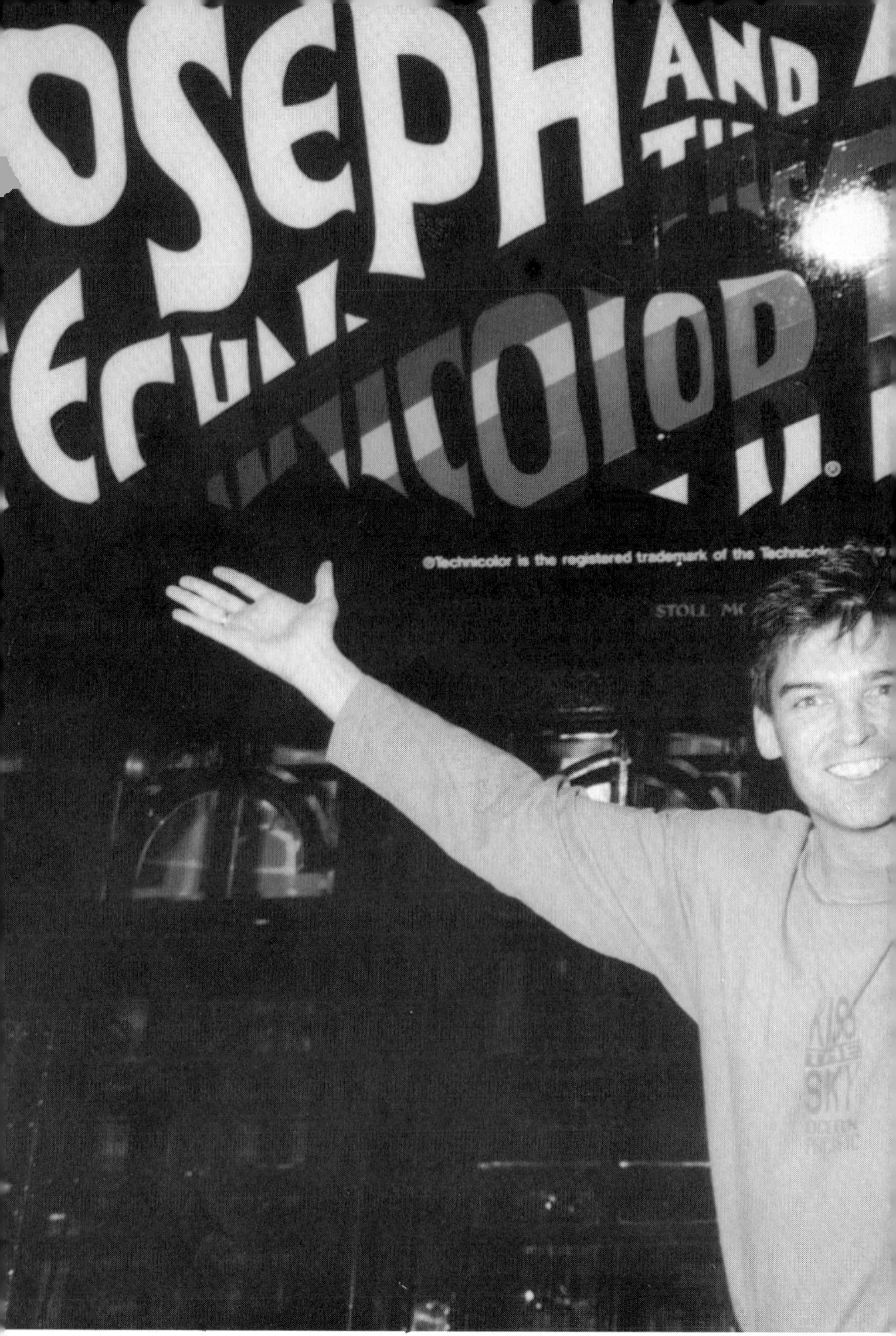
AND
®Technicolor is the registered trademark of the

With the amazing Andrew Lloyd-Webber.

to print money – and the chance to make their number-one client a superstar.

Phil recalled: 'I was absolutely gobsmacked. I thought the first half had gone pretty well and I hadn't made any big errors. But the last thing I expected Andrew to say was that.'

The immediate effect of the news was that Phillip went back out for the second half on cloud nine. He floated through the set, gaining confidence and cheekiness as it went on. By the time he finished, the audience were whipped into a frenzy of excitement. He topped the atmosphere with a brilliant encore of 'Any Dream Will Do'.

As a hydraulic cage winched him up to the royal circle, Phil looked for his friends and family. And he looked particularly for one person – Mum Pat.

He remembers: 'It was the most emotional, exciting, thrilling moment of my entire life. As I was raised higher and higher towards where the folks were sitting I could see the whole audience on their feet cheering and clapping.

'Then I spotted Mum and she was crying with joy. That totally threw me. I felt tears well up inside me and I was convinced I was going to burst out crying. My lips started quivering and my legs went to jelly. Seeing the people I love most looking so proud and happy for me was a wonderful experience.'

When he finally landed back on stage for a last bow his fellow cast members lifted him on to their shoulders to take a five-minute standing ovation.

An hour later, he had showered and changed into a smart suit to join a select group of friends and family at his favourite hotel, the Langham Hilton opposite the Radio One studios in Regent Street.

Sarah Greene and husband Mike Smith were there, Russ Lindsay and his wife Caron Keating, Caron's mum Gloria

Hunniford, Peter Powell and his wife Anthea Turner. And Pat, Brian and Tim Schofield. There was also one other very special young lady: Phil's new girlfriend Stephanie.

Sipping champagne to the accompaniment of French music, Phil made a brief, emotional speech. He said it had been the greatest moment of his life, and thanked them all for their support and help. Most of all, he said, he'd like to thank his parents. Brian and Pat stood by his side glowing with pride.

She said: 'Both my sons have given me so much to be proud about, but tonight was a bit special. I couldn't believe how good Phil was. I had seen Jason in *Joseph* so I knew what to expect, but seeing him singing like that was wonderful, wonderful.

'He's been a smashing son to me, the best any mother could wish for. He keeps in touch all the time and travels down to see us in Newquay as often as he can. He never lets things go to his head and tonight won't either. Phil will just take it all in his stride – he is so modest about his achievements.'

Dad Brian was equally effusive. 'He was grand tonight, really grand. We are all so pleased for his success – he deserves it all.'

Phil spent the next hour by the side of his blonde girl-friend. They kissed, cuddled and whispered in each other's ears. It was obvious to anyone there that he was hopelessly in love.

As the Schofield party left at 1 am, Phil bade an emotional and very personal farewell to each and everyone there.

'Now we will just have to see how the reviews are,' he said.

He needn't have worried. The papers were unanimous – he was a smash.

Leading the way was the *Sun* – which made Phil's trium-

...rtying with Andrew Lloyd-Webber after the first performance of Joseph.

To the victor go the cuddles! With Mike Smith and Sarah Greene.

Receiving yet another award. This time from Piers Morgan,
Sun columnist and author of this book.

phant debut its lead story on the front page with the head-line: 'PHIL's BRILL!' The report said Phillip had been a 'stunning success' and predicted a 'spectacular future' for him.

Other papers agreed. The *Mirror* said his performance was 'astonishing'. The *Daily Mail's* Baz Bamigboye reported: 'Mr Schofield was a charming success.'

By mid-afternoon the next day, most of Britain was talking about him. Phillip had become a superstar.

Andrew Lloyd-Webber said: 'What can I say? Phillip proved tonight that he can perform superbly on stage. I knew he could do it and he did. I am delighted that other people think he is as good as I do. I think we will be seeing a lot more of him in the future.'